Original title:
A Sapling's Soliloquy

Copyright © 2025 Creative Arts Management OÜ
All rights reserved.

Author: Lila Davenport
ISBN HARDBACK: 978-1-80567-323-1
ISBN PAPERBACK: 978-1-80567-622-5

Sunlit Aspirations

In the morning, I stretch wide,
Reaching high, with leafy pride.
Birds fly by, chirping loud,
I call back, feeling proud!

Sunshine smiles upon my face,
Worms below play a silly race.
A gentle sway, I dance and twirl,
Nature's stage, I give a whirl!

Rain drops come, each a tiny splash,
I giggle as they make a crash.
Mud below, a sloppy mess,
I wear it like a fancy dress!

So here I stand, with dreams in tow,
In this grand show, I'm the star in the glow.
With roots so deep, my spirit's free,
Oh, who knew nature could be so silly?

Dreams from a Decomposing Leaf

Once I danced on branches high,
Now I lie and slowly sigh.
A colorful past, not to forget,
Regrets? Nah, just a leafy pet!

Bugs crawl by, a tiny parade,
Their munching sounds, a leafy serenade.
I crack a joke, 'I'm not dead yet!'
Life's a feast, don't you fret!

As the wind whispers, I giggle too,
Missing the sun, but still feeling blue.
With nature's laugh, I give a chat,
To worms nearby, and they just sat!

So here I lay, I don't complain,
A leaf's wise words can entertain.
Even in decay, there's fun to find,
In every layer, stories intertwined!

Voices of the Awakening Nature

Morning calls with chirps and hoots,
Squirrels chase in tiny boots.
'Time to rise!' the flowers chime,
A garden song in perfect rhyme!

Bouncing bunnies hop around,
With floppy ears, they make no sound.
Sunbeams dance on blades of grass,
'What a party!' the critters pass!

A stream nearby drops a beat,
With pebbles clapping, it's quite a treat!
While frogs join in with croaky tunes,
Nature's jamming under the moons!

So voices rise with morning light,
Each creature bold, each spirit bright.
In the great outdoors, all is right,
Let's laugh together, what a sight!

Growing Pains and Promises

Hunched down low, I feel the strain,
Reaching up, it's a funny game!
Roots stretch wide, seeking snacks,
Oh, to find life's hidden tracks!

Stretching, yawning, what a sight,
Neighbors tease, 'You're not so bright!'
Yet, I bloom with quirky flair,
My colors wild, beyond compare!

Bumbling bugs keep buzzing near,
Could it be I'm their biggest cheer?
With every poke and little nudge,
I laugh out loud, 'What a grudge!'

Although I stumble through this phase,
Each leafy day brings fun-filled ways.
Embracing growth with silly grins,
In this wild life, who really wins?

The Promise Held in Tiny Leaves

In a pot with dreams so grand,
I wiggle my roots for a chance at land.
I'll grow tall and never tire,
But first, I need some water to inspire!

The sun peeks down, a golden tease,
Hey leaf buddies, can you feel the breeze?
Let's dance around and catch some rays,
We'll plot a takeover in funny ways!

Breaths Beneath the Surface

Underneath the soil, I giggle small,
Listening to raindrops like a curtain call.
Oh to break free from this earthy embrace,
And stretch my limbs in a sunlit race!

My neighbors, the worms, share gossip with flair,
They wiggle and squirm without any care.
Earthworms unite, together we scheme,
To hatch a plan and grow tall—what a dream!

Voices of Nature's Tenderness

The sparrows sing sweetly, not quite in tune,
While I chuckle softly at their odd little croon.
A squirrel runs by, all fluff and delight,
I might just narrate his next acorn flight!

Beneath my green, I hear whispers of fun,
Every rustle and creak makes my day run.
Nature's a stage with a quirky twist,
Where every creature plays a role on the list.

Glimpses of a Bud's Desire

A bud I remain, with dreams oh so grand,
Wishing for petals to bloom on command.
 Why is it a crime to just want to peek?
The wait is a riot, but I'm feeling cheeky!

 I see bees in a hurry, oh what a sight,
Buzzing around, pretending to take flight.
 I'll pop out soon, with colors so bright,
And join in their antics, with sheer delight!

The Soul's Search for Sunlight

In a pot, I sit so snug,
Hoping I'll be free, not tugged.
The sun peeks down, a golden ray,
"Hey, up here!" I shout, "Hooray!"

Strained my leaves to reach the glow,
But all I touch is dirt below.
The ants just laugh; they think it's sweet,
Yet I just want a little heat!

Chasing rays with all my might,
Dodging shadows, oh what a fight!
"Grow tall!" I hear the wise ones say,
I just want a sunlit buffet!

Seasons shift, I stretch my arms,
Dreaming of the sun's warm charms.
"Time to grow, just take the chance!"
Maybe I'll get my sun-kissed dance!

The Gentle Growing Voice

Little whispers stir the ground,
Dreams of heights where I'm unbound.
"Grow big, grow tall, don't be shy!"
Yet all I do is question why.

The worms sing songs of mud and rain,
I sigh and giggle at my own disdain.
"Oh to bloom!" I softly beam,
While pondering leaves and a grander scheme.

My roots are deep, but oh, the wait,
I watch the world, it seems so great.
With every sprout, there's strength in jest,
For even plants must take their rest.

One day I'll stretch to greet the stars,
Perhaps with some friends, and a few guitars.
But for now, I'll hum my tune,
As crazy dreams float past the moon!

From Seed to Dream

Started out so small and round,
Tucked away beneath the ground.
Worms told tales of sunlight's grace,
And little dreams began to race.

When the rain came down in sheets,
I danced around with tiny feats.
"Just grow, you silly little thing!"
I heard the breeze, and it made me sing.

One poke of light, a little boo!
I yielded roots and branches too.
"Look at me!" I proudly boast,
But still miss mom's warm sunshine toast.

Adventures wait in every leaf,
I'll tell the world, beyond belief.
With joy I sprout, let laughter ring,
From seed to dream, I'm blossoming!

Reflections of a New Beginning

In the mirror of a dew-kissed blade,
I see my future, unafraid.
Reflections tease with every glint,
"You'll grow strong, don't you squint!"

The early birds come chirping near,
I laugh at them, I have no fear.
They think they're wise, oh what a jest,
But I'm the one who's on a quest!

Across the garden, whispers fly,
"Look at little me, I'll touch the sky!"
With every inch, my roots dig deep,
While visions of grandeur make me leap.

So here I stand, bright and aware,
With silly hopes beyond compare.
New beginnings every day anew,
I'm just a sprout with dreams to pursue!

The Unfolding of a Leafy Soul

In the silence of the garden, I sway,
Hoping to catch a breeze today.
But with such glee, I'm stuck in place,
Guess I'll just dance with the bugs in my space.

Sunlight's warm, my mission is clear,
Photosynthesis? Let's give a cheer!
Yet, I wonder why the ants think me tall,
When I'm just trying not to fall.

Each raindrop's a party, drumming on my head,
Bubbles of joy sent from the sky, I'm fed.
Yet, when the wind whispers, I lose my pact,
Is it too much fun to stay intact?

Oh, to grow up strong, I'd like to boast,
But I must admit, I'm still quite a ghost.
With roots so deep, but dreams so grand,
I might just be the silliest in this land.

The Tenderest Thoughts of Burgeoning Life

With each sunrise, I stretch out wide,
Thinking of all that lives inside.
What if I were to wear a crown?
A leafy hat to never look down!

The worms below say, 'Grow more roots!'
But I shout back, 'I want cute boots!'
Imagine me, swagging with style,
A plant superstar, walking a mile.

The breeze is my friend, but at times is a tease,
It messes my hair, oh, such a breeze!
I dream of flowers, colors so bright,
Just to show off a dazzling sight.

Yet, in the shadows, a shadow does loom,
A squirrel eyeing my space, bringing doom.
But I giggle and think, 'He's got to be crazy,'
For I'm the sassiest leaf, never too hazy!

Secrets Whispered in Quiet Shadows

In the shade, I hear it all,
Crickets gossip, with their tiny call.
They speak of grass and what's in fashion,
Who's the fastest? Oh, the sass and passion!

The daisies blush, they think they're sleek,
While I sneak a glance; I'm too shy to peek.
However, I think I might have a shot,
To steal some sunlight, at least, why not?

There's a frog in the pond with dreams of song,
Croaking loudly, he thinks he's strong.
But little do they know, I'm here to stay,
With my leafy wit, I'll laugh every day.

So secrets, not just mine, shall we share?
Under the moon with the cool, brisk air.
I'm learning to bloom, to dodge and weave,
And write my own tale, oh, how to believe!

Musings of a Branch in Bloom

Here I am, a branch with dreams,
Blossoms and buds, and cute little themes.
What if I dance like no one cares?
Will my flowers bloom and flaunt their wares?

Sometimes, I ponder, do birds think I'm sweet?
When they land on me, do they leave their feet?
I try to impress with my vibrant hues,
Hoping they pick me to show off their views!

Each whimsy wind tickles my bark,
I sway and shake as it makes its mark.
The bees buzz loudly, a laugh in the air,
Do they think I'm their style? Oh, what a scare!

And when night falls, and stars start to sway,
I giggle with leaves, 'Let's dance and play!'
For in this world of sunshine and gloom,
It's best to enjoy when we get to bloom!

Conversations with the Wind

Oh breeze, do tell me, why do you sway?
You dance with the leaves, but never do stay.
Whisper your secrets, I'm eager to hear,
Are you just spinning tall tales, my dear?

You tickle my branches and ruffle my hair,
With giggles and wiggles, I'm light as a flare.
But when you grow gusty, I wobble and bend,
Oh windy companion, are we near the end?

You tease me with tales of the big, wide blue,
Of mountains and valleys and skies so true.
Yet still here I stand, rooted and small,
Are you sure I'll grow up to be one and all?

So whisper your secrets, oh whimsical gale,
Let's plot my bright future, over a tall tale.
We'll giggle and wriggle until the day's done,
Together we'll dream of the heights we might run.

Yearning for the Rain

Oh, clouds up above, are you plotting a scheme?
You tease us with shadows and make me just dream.
I wiggle my leaves, I sway to and fro,
But without your sweet sprinkle, my thirst starts to grow.

With hope in my heart, I shout to the sky,
"Please drop just a drizzle, I'm asking you, why?"
But all I get back is a puff of dry air,
A sprinkle of silence—oh, how can this bear?

You rumble and tumble, I dance while I wait,
The ants have all gathered, oh is it my fate?
To sing without water and chatter like this?
Oh rain, why oh why do you make me wish?

So while I stand small, with a thirst loud and bright,
My dreams fill with puddles, oh what a grand sight!
I chuckle and wiggle, my leaves they still sway,
For surely one day, I must get my bouquet!

The Journey of a Tiny Stem

I ventured from soil, a brave little sprout,
With a wobbly wave and a curious shout.
"Watch out world, here I come, hold on tight!"
But a leaf told me, "You're not ready for flight!"

I stumbled and fumbled, I twirled in the breeze,
Twirling and swirling, I did it with ease!
"A tumble!" I laughed as I fell on the ground,
The worms all cheered—now that's a fine sound!

Each day I grow taller, but man, what a chore,
Dodging the bugs that keep knocking at my door.
"Hey there, my friend, can you kindly refrain?"
I giggle and wiggle, trying hard to remain.

But on this wild journey, with giggles galore,
I'll conquer the garden, and then I'll explore!
So watch out, dear world, as I stretch and I shine,
This tiny stem's here, and it's all by design!

Unseen Beneath the Surface

Underneath the ground, where the critters roam free,
Lies a world full of wonders, oh can't you see?
I wiggle my roots in the dirt, what a treat!
It's a party of fungi and bugs—what a feat!

The snails and the beetles, they chatter and brag,
While the worms put on shows in their little dirt flag.
"Oh, what a fine place for a root to unwind!"
I chuckle to myself, feeling quite well-defined.

The whispers of soil are the best kind of cheer,
"We'll help you grow big, just be patient, my dear!"
I surge through the darkness, a quest without fright,
"Just sprinkle some water, and I'll dance in the light!"

So here in the shadows, we giggle and play,
While dreaming of sunlight, we wish it would stay.
With laughter and joy, beneath layers we thrive,
In this hidden haven, we feel so alive!

Dreams in the Salt of the Earth

In soil I sit with dreams so neat,
I wonder if worms think life is sweet.
My leaves have plans to dance and sway,
But the sun keeps throwing shade my way.

A bird drops by to make a jest,
"You're just a snack; not much, but rest!"
I giggle back, my roots held tight,
"Watch me grow tall! You'll see my height!"

With ants my friends in this tiny zone,
They march around like they own the throne.
I'll stretch and grow, oh woe is me,
Earth's a funny place for a small tree.

So here I stand with hopes so grand,
What's up ahead? A leafy band?
Wishing on stars with my sprouty crew,
In dreams of salt, I'll grow anew!

Serenade of Soft New Fronds

Oh, soft fronds sway in a breezy tune,
With critters lounging beneath the moon.
Whispering secrets to friends in the dirt,
While my roots tickle the toes of a shirt.

A ladybug hums, with rhythm divine,
"Grow tall enough, and you'll sip wine!"
I chuckle softly, my leaves all a-fluff,
"Will it be red or just garden stuff?"

The bumbles buzzing around my base,
Cracking jokes, but oh, what a race!
As I stretch up, they tease with a grin,
"Just keep your cool, you're bound to win!"

So here I play in this verdant spree,
To serenade the sun and glee.
Such joy in roots, I'll dance without fear,
With soft new fronds, happy and near!

Small Voice in a World of Giants

In a world so big, I'm quite the sprout,
Whispering hopes, what's this all about?
The clouds just laugh as they float real high,
"Stay small, little one! Just say goodbye!"

Yet here I stand with a grin so wide,
Does anyone hear my leafy pride?
The daisies chuckle, my pals at play,
"Grow tall if you can, but not today!"

Grass blades tease, they wiggle with flair,
Ah, but this sapling has dreams to spare.
I'll stretch and dance, let the currents lead,
In a world of giants, watch this small seed!

For every giant must start so small,
With dreams and laughter—oof, I might fall!
But I'll rise up, let the joy unfurl,
In a small voice echoing through the world!

The Hopes that Reach Skyward

Beneath the sky, my hopes take flight,
While aiming high, I wonder, "Is this right?"
My branches stretch, a comical sight,
Chasing the clouds in their fluffy white.

A squirrel sits high, gives me a wink,
"Reach for the stars, come on, don't blink!"
I laugh, "Just one? My tips feel the strain!
Can I stretch more without going insane?"

With whispers of dreams in the summer's air,
I twirl and twist without a care.
The raindrops giggle, all soft and round,
Turning my hopes to excitement unbound.

So here I stand, hopes rolling in glee,
With every quirk, I want to be free.
To dance, to twirl, and wiggle up high,
With hopes that reach skyward, oh how I try!

Dreams in the Dappled Light

In a world of soil and cheer,
I wonder what I might become,
A flower or a tree so dear,
Or just a garden's silly hum.

The sun shines bright, my leaves stretch wide,
I wriggle here, I wiggle there,
A worm's my friend, we're side by side,
Sharing secrets in the air.

With every raindrop that descends,
I giggle as my roots go deep,
I dream of branches, twisty bends,
But nap first, it's time to sleep!

The butterflies, they stop and stare,
"My, what a funny shape you've got!"
I wink and wave without a care,
"Thanks, my friend, I can't be caught!"

Seedling's Musings

Nestled snug in cozy dirt,
I ponder life beneath the sun,
Will I wear petals or a shirt?
Oh, the fun has just begun!

The breeze whispers a gentle tale,
Of dancing leaves and skies so blue,
I might just sprout and set my sail,
Adventure calls—it's true!

A squirrel passes, thinks I'm neat,
He chuckles at my little height,
"Short and stout, you can't compete!"
But I'll outgrow him, what a sight!

So here I stand, with dreams so bright,
In the garden's corner, I await,
With every inch, I feel the light,
Oh, how I love to contemplate!

The Unfolding Leaf

As I unfurl my leafy cloak,
What surprises will I see?
A shady nook, or a wise oak?
Maybe friends from the bumblebee!

Each rustle brings a joke or two,
I laugh with every swaying breeze,
Kissing petals, thought I'd grew,
Who knew I'd have such good tease?

"Hey, look at me!" the winds will call,
I shimmy to their playful tune,
Though I'm small, I'm having a ball,
Dancing 'neath the smiling moon!

With morning light, I'll spin and sway,
A leaf ballet beyond compare,
In nature's theater, come what may,
I'll find my joy in the open air!

Echoes from the Earth

Beneath the surface, stories sleep,
Whispers of the past come near,
Do roots really laughingly creep?
Let's shout it out for all to hear!

I hear the tales of fallen leaves,
They tickle my toes when they sigh,
Like gossiping friends, oh how it weaves,
Past seasons laugh as they float by!

The laughter of raindrops is sweet,
On my head, they fall and play,
Can water bugs dance on my feet?
Oh, let me join in! Hip hip hooray!

Above, the clouds rumble and cheer,
A thunderous giggle breaks the calm,
Each echo from the earth, my dear,
Is just a funny woodland psalm!

A Young Tree's Quiet Thoughts

Why do squirrels dart and play?
They dance like nuts, all day!
Do they know I'm stuck right here?
I'd trade my leaves for some cold beer!

Birds sit high and make a mess,
To me, they're quite the stress.
They chirp about their grand old flight,
While I just wait—oh what a plight!

Shadow friends, the weeds, do tease,
Dare them dance? Oh, what a breeze!
With roots so deep, I stand my ground,
But in my dreams, I fly around!

So here I grow, won't outgrow cheer,
With funny thoughts, I persevere.
For life as green as grass can be,
Shall have a laugh right here with me!

The Green Heart's Whisper

I thought I'd grow to touch the sun,
But I'm just here having fun!
Beetles marching in a line,
Tell me tales of food and wine.

The wind shouts with all its might,
It yells of storms that start at night.
But maybe it just wants to play,
And toss my leaves all night and day!

A raccoon winks, with mischief sly,
Says he'll help me reach the sky!
But all he brings is socks and trash,
I roll my eyes; oh what a clash!

Still, I laugh through the ups and downs,
With muddy boots and silly frowns.
This leafy life is quite a treat,
With joyous roots beneath my feet!

Musings Under Moonlit Canopy

Under stars, I ponder fate,
What's in store for me? I wait.
The moon looks down with a gleeful grin,
Whispers secrets to the wind within.

My branches stretch like silly arms,
Try to frame the gnome with charms.
But all he does is giggle low,
And then pops popcorn 'til I glow!

In midnight dances, shadows twirl,
Squirrels conduct, oh what a whirl!
Leaves rustle with laughter, a comical spree,
I wish for all to come laugh with me!

As night unfolds with playful glee,
I welcome joy, strong and free.
For in this forest, we all belong,
Together, humor sings its song!

A Journey into the Light

I sprouted up with dreams so tall,
Yet here I am, against a wall.
A chipmunk whispers, 'Just hang tight!'
'We'll travel far, just hold on tight!'

The sun pokes through with flair so bright,
Baking me like toast, what a plight!
A butterfly flits, so grand and spry,
I wonder if it'd teach me to fly?

But then it flies to nibble blooms,
Leaving me here in a world of fumes.
I chuckle to roots, 'What's our plan?'
A worm pops up, 'Let's start a band!'

And so we groove, a leafy crew,
With shadows dancing, oh what's new?
We sway and laugh through every plight,
On this odd journey, full of light!

The Fledgling's Yearn for the Sky

In the pot, I sit and sigh,
Stretching leaves to the azure high.
A bird scoffs, as if to tease,
"You're stuck, my friend, on ground like peas!"

With roots that wiggle, I thrash about,
Estimating climbs without a doubt.
"If I could leap, I'd touch the clouds,
But here I stay, among the crowds!"

So many dreams wrapped in green,
To be the tallest, so it seems.
But squirrels mock with their high hops,
While I just sway, and hope it stops!

One day I'll stand, oh, just you wait!
To reach the sun, that's my fate.
And all the critters will be saying,
"Look at that tree, what a displaying!"

Chilling Dreams of a Mellow Morning

Morning dew, a chilly glance,
Dreams of warmth, I take a chance.
A breeze comes by, gives me a nudge,
"You won't grow up if you can't budge!"

A snail slithers, oh so slow,
"Doing laps? Just take it slow."
I laugh and wish I could be fast,
But rooted here, my dreams amass.

At breakfast time, the sun peeks in,
While worms groove under my skin.
"Don't be shy," the sunbeam beams,
"Join the dance, embrace your dreams!"

Tick-tock, trees, the time will go,
Soon enough, I'll steal the show.
And as I sway, I'll steal the scene,
With funky moves, the sprout machine!

Soliloquy of Sun-Drenched Green

Lying low on sun-kissed ground,
My leaves stretch wide, it feels profound.
"Oops, not too far!" I laugh and sway,
Leaves tickling bugs who thought they'd stay.

"Hey, Mr. Ant, come dance with me!"
"Not today, you move too free!"
I giggle as they scamper back,
Didn't know I'd cause a hack!

I bask in rays, it's quite divine,
Chasing shadows, feeling fine.
But watch this dance, I call my own,
While bees buzz by, I'm never alone.

Soon I'll rise, this sprout shall shine,
With roots and dreams that intertwine.
In a world of wiggly fun,
I'm here to grow, I'm here to run!

Awareness of the World Above

What's that sound? A raucous crow!
He flaps and flouts, puts on a show.
"Bet you can't fly as good as me!"
"I'll show you soon; just let me be!"

The sky's a rink, and I'm the skater,
Hoping to glide, a dream creator.
But here I stay, a grounded treat,
With wiggles and wriggles from my feet.

Oh, the drama of leaf and stem,
While bees argue like a busy gem.
"Did you taste that flower's nectar sweet?"
"Oh yes, my friend, a fragrant feat!"

But soon enough, I'll join the fray,
And dance with birds at end of day.
Beneath the stars, I'll hold my ground,
A real tall tale, oh, so profound!

Thoughts of a Little Leaf

Swinging freely on a twig,
I ponder life, a tiny gig.
Why do worries fall like dew?
Just ride the breeze, the sky's so blue.

Sunbeams tickle, wind takes hold,
I laugh at storms, I'm brave and bold.
Do I care if birds fly near?
Not when I've got jokes to share!

Frolicking in the morning light,
With every giggle, I take flight.
What's for breakfast? Just some air!
Life's a party, come and share!

Though I'm small, I spread good cheer,
In rustling whispers, lend an ear.
With a dance, I greet each day,
Oh, how I love to laugh and play!

Ramblings of Roots in Darkness

Down below in soil so deep,
We chit-chat while others sleep.
What's the gossip? Oh, it's grand,
The earth's full secrets, close at hand.

Tickle me, a worm pops by,
Back and forth, we laugh and sigh.
Why did that seed cross the bed?
To sprout a dream, it said, it said!

The rocks around have stories too,
Like, 'Why am I not green like you?'
We root for each, our tangled ties,
In this cool place where laughter lies.

We scheme and plot for light above,
Though we're hidden, we're crushed with love.
Deep down here, it's fun for free,
Join the party, roots and me!

The Fragile Leap of Life

From a bud, I stretch and curl,
With a bounce, I start to twirl.
A leap of faith, what could go wrong?
Just watch me grooving to nature's song.

I wibble, wobble, sway with ease,
The world is big; I feel the breeze.
Do I fear a fall to the ground?
Not when fun is all around!

Catch me if you can, I tease,
My tiny dance, a little freeze.
The sky's my stage, and clouds applaud,
With a spin, I shout, "I'm not a fraud!"

I twirl and twist, 'til evening's near,
My fragile leap, so full of cheer.
So come along, let's take a chance,
Life's a jig; let's join the dance!

Meditation of the Earth Below

Hold your breath, let's think of dirt,
A cozy home, where roots can flirt.
We giggle low, in shadows cast,
Life's a riddle, oh how it's vast!

Listen close, the whispers crawl,
Earth's little secrets call to all.
From acorns' dreams to mushrooms' jest,
We ponder life and gather zest.

Each little rock has tales to tell,
Of goofy bugs and lilting smells.
With our laughter, we softly shake,
Find joy in every wormy break!

Hold hands with moss, the snuggly bed,
Where thoughts of fluffy dreams are spread.
Beneath the surface, joy does thrive,
In the earth's womb, we come alive!

Whispers of the Young Oak

In the breeze, I dance and sway,
Roots tickle toes where I play.
Don't mind the squirrels, they're just my pals,
Stashing acorns like they're in some dells.

Sunshine's flair, my leafy crown,
Pulling faces, never a frown.
Watch me grow, I'm quite the sight,
Saluting clouds with all my might.

On rainy days, I might complain,
But a puddle's my personal train.
Splashing round, I giggle and grin,
Nature's stage where I begin.

So here I stand, less than a tree,
Full of dreams and silly glee.
With every inch, I feel so spry,
A little oak under the vast sky.

In the Shade of Tomorrow

Beneath my leaves, secrets thrive,
Whispers of bugs, they come alive.
Calling all creatures, come take a seat,
We'll share stories, oh what a treat!

Bees hum songs of golden delight,
While I stretch, feeling quite light.
The sun peeks in, a cheeky show,
"Hey there, little guy, how'd you grow?"

At night I dream of stars so bright,
Plotting adventures in moonlight.
If I could dance, I'd surely prance,
Swirling with shadows, what a chance!

In the future, I'll touch the sky,
For now, I just watch the birds fly by.
With every gust, I giggle and shake,
Growing up for fun's dear sake.

The Quiet Voice of Green

They call me quiet, but hear my cheer,
In the rustle, you'll find me near.
Little whispers from my leafy lips,
Join in the fun, let's play some flips!

Each raindrop's a tickle on my head,
A tiny dance party instead.
I sway and shimmer in the breeze,
Life's a joke; oh, what a tease!

Acorns drop like tiny bombs,
With each plop, a giggle comes.
Nature's pranks keep me on my toes,
You think I'm small? Just wait, who knows!

In the company of critters, I thrive,
Creating laughter, oh what a drive.
With roots in the ground and dreams in the air,
I'm the liveliest green with a flair!

Roots of Reflection

My roots speak truths, oh so wise,
In the soil, under starlit skies.
They tell me tales of ancient trees,
Who danced with the wind, with such ease!

I sit in silence, pondering life,
Imagining adventures, free from strife.
If I'd just sprout some wings one day,
I'd soar high and find my way!

Oh, the creatures laugh at my dreams,
But I know there's more than it seems.
With each wriggle of my tiny root,
I'll grow and grow; who'll hold my suit?

So hear me chuckle, takes a while,
For a little sprout, I've got my style.
In this vibrant world, full of cheer,
I'll dance and shine throughout the year!

Cries of the New Green Dawn

In the morning light I stand,
Shaking off the night so grand,
Whispering to the passing breeze,
"Can a leaf ever catch a sneeze?"

With sunshine tickling my new leaves,
I giggle at the buzzing bees,
They dance around in silly flight,
While I just stretch with all my might.

Oh, how the clouds above do float,
I wonder if they wear a coat,
Sometimes I wish for wings to fly,
But then I'd miss the worms nearby!

With roots so deep, I stay secure,
The world outside seems less than pure,
Yet here I wave my tiny arms,
In hopes they notice all my charms!

Musings from the Heart of the Soil

Buried deep, my thoughts take root,
Trapped between some old, stinky boot,
I ponder life just a little too,
Like, do ants dream? And if they do?

Each time the rain falls with a splash,
I laugh and wiggle, what a splash!
The gophers giggle from their hide,
As I recall my sprout-filled pride.

Every worm here seems a bit strange,
They wiggle around, never change,
But one day, when the sun comes out,
I'll show them all what life's about!

In the dark, I might seem shy,
Yet I practice my dance and sigh,
When the roots grab hold and wiggle,
I giggle—oh, how the world does jiggle!

The Unseen Struggles Underground

Beneath the surface, we all fight,
A battle for the sun's warm light,
In silence, we stretch and bend,
Competing with the weeds, my friend.

The rocks are heavy, oh so rude,
Interrupting my leafy mood,
But I push back with all my might,
And whisper softly, "Not tonight!"

The critters scurry, causing fear,
With little paws and tiny sneers,
But I just chuckle and stand tall,
For someday soon, I'll grace them all!

Each struggle turns into a jest,
I'll grow so high, they'll be impressed,
With branches dancing in the breeze,
No longer hiding from the tease!

The Yearning of a Budding Dream

Oh, to be more than just a sprout,
A towering tree, there's no doubt,
I dream each day while sipping dew,
Of squirrels laughing, joining too.

But here I am, just in my zone,
Wishing I could find a throne,
And yet I hear the daisies jest,
"Just grow up, and you shall be blessed!"

With every inch, I shout with glee,
I twirl and twist, so wild and free,
If dreams come true, prepare the stage,
For I'm the star—just check my page!

I might be small, but not in heart,
With every leaf, I'll play my part,
So watch out world, I'll reach the sky,
With dreams so big, I'll surely fly!

In Pursuit of the Sun

I stretch my leaves to greet the dawn,
In search of rays, I think I'm drawn.
The sun is bright, my sneaky friend,
But oh, the shade, it won't quite end!

I lean and twist, a dance I weave,
With branches swaying, what a reprieve!
The bees are laughing, buzzing loud,
While I just mumble, feeling proud.

With every inch I climb and bend,
A toddler's tantrum, I'll pretend.
To grow or not, that's my big quest,
If I could only, I'd take a rest!

Yet still I rise, through earth I creep,
In this funny game, I just can't sleep!
With sunshine's warmth and friendly air,
I'll keep on growing without a care!

Tales of Tender Growth

In a garden chat, I gossip free,
With busy ants who drink their tea.
They share the gossip of the day,
But all I want is to swing and sway!

Each raindrop falls like nature's song,
While I complain, "This won't take long!"
I hug the dirt, my cozy bed,
While plotting out my growth instead.

A worm once teased, 'You're just a sprout!'
I faked a laugh, but felt some doubt.
Yet as I grew, I stood up high,
"Who's the tiny one now?" I cry!

With tales of giggles and some grace,
I'll tell the world, my happy place.
With each new leaf, I'll paint a scene,
Of life's big dance, it's quite the dream!

Murmurs from the Soil

Beneath the ground, the whispers flow,
I listen close, but don't quite know.
A potato said, 'Let's learn to roll!'
While carrots chuckle, digging their hole.

The earthworms wiggle in pure delight,
While roots complain of cramped insight.
I nudge and poke, a tiny tease,
'Come join the fun, oh roots with ease!'

Underneath the cozy clover,
I watch the world, my little cover.
The soil is warm, a blanket's hug,
But I can't wait to give a shrug!

So here I stand, a little poke,
With every giggle, I'll break the yoke.
Soon I'll burst out and say, "Ta-da!"
With all my friends, hurrah, hurrah!

A Bud's Longing

I'm just a bud, not much to see,
But wait, there's magic, just for me!
With every tick of nature's clock,
I dream of blooming, oh what a shock!

In secret nights, I plot and scheme,
To burst forth bright—a wildflower dream.
The garden talks, old tales they swap,
"Don't fret, dear bud, you'll dance and hop!"

A bumblebee buzzes, full of cheer,
"Join the party, it's happening here!"
I stretch my leaves, give a little shake,
Could this be real? Make no mistake!

The day will come, I'll show my flair,
With colors bright, I'll fill the air.
Till then I giggle, hide, and wait,
For fabulous blooms—I can hardly wait!

Reflections of Morning Dew

I woke up with a drop or two,
Feeling fresh like the morning brew.
The world looks grand, it's all so bright,
But wait—what's that? A bird in flight!

My leaves are dancing with the breeze,
Trying hard to act like me, please!
But every gust makes me wobble, too,
Oh, silly me, just a morning dew!

Tales of Fluttering Roots

My roots are restless, can't stay still,
They chat about the grass on the hill.
Who knew soil could be such a gossip?
I'm rooted here, but my dreams just flop!

In the dark, they whisper and tease,
"Stretch, my friend! It'll be a breeze!"
But tangled tales trip me up each day,
Next time, I'll keep my roots at bay!

Yearnings of a Young Trunk

Here I stand, trying to grow tall,
Yet every time, I feel so small.
The older trees, they laugh and grin,
They're giants, while I'm just a pin!

I long to reach the skies so blue,
But every squirrel says, "Not yet, dude!"
Some say I'm just a twig in wait,
But I've got dreams that won't abate!

Seasons of Sprout and Sun

Spring arrives, it's time to sprout,
Let's have a party, that's what I shout!
But bees start buzzing, oh what a fright,
"Just hang tight, kid, we'll take flight!"

Summer's sun makes me want to dance,
But who knew leaves could be so prance?
I wave to clouds, they bring the rain,
"Stop tickling me, you're such a pain!"

As autumn colors start to blaze,
I'm making plans and counting days.
Yet here comes winter, full of frost,
Oh well, I'll nap now, at a cost!

Confessions of a Rooted Heart

I tried to grow tall, but I'm stuck down here,
With worms for friends and no one to cheer.
The squirrels throw acorns, oh what a splat!
I dream of the sun, but I wear a hat.

The grass mocks my height, it's a real shame,
While daisies and daisies play flower games.
I whisper sweet nothings to passing bees,
Who buzz in my ears, 'Get up, if you please!'

I'm jealous of ferns, so leafy and bright,
While I'm in the shadows, without any light.
I sigh at the flowers that dance in the breeze,
While I talk to ants and exchange memes with trees.

But who needs to stretch when I've got a view,
Of all the mishaps that the garden crew do?
I laugh through the seasons, with roots in the dirt,
In this tangled-up mess, I'm the king of the hurt!

Learning from the Dance of Leaves

Oh, the leaves are twirling, how do they do that?
While I'm just here, making friends with a cat.
They spin and they swirl, not a worry or care,
While I'm stuck in the mud, with muck in my hair.

It's a leafy ballet, oh what a fine scene,
With acorns as props and a pine tree as queen.
I call out, 'Hey leaves, can you teach me the tricks?'
But they just laugh back, saying, 'You need some kicks!'

I'd join in their frolic, but it's hard to get up,
With this great wooden trunk, I'm a sturdy old pup.
They tease me a lot, yet I make them all laugh,
When I sway to the wind like a clumsy giraffe.

Still, watching their waltz makes my heart feel so light,
As they paint the whole garden in colors so bright.
So I'll sit here and chuckle, and take notes on the breeze,
'Cause maybe one day, I'll too join their tease!'

Solitude in the Shade of Giants

Here I am stuck, in the shade of the old,
With friends like these, I'm feeling quite bold.
The beech and the oak, oh, they're so very wise,
While I share my stories with chipmunks who rise.

I pose like a statue while they prattle and preach,
While I'm learning the gossip, they're out of my reach.
It's lonely down here, but wait, here comes a bug,
With a wink and a nod, it gives me a shrug.

I'll just stay nestled, in my cozy old nook,
Gleaning their secrets, writing my book.
With roots deep in gossip, I'm not feeling shy,
Who needs tall friends when you can just lie?

So let them tower, with their branches so grand,
I've got all the dirt, my own little band.
In shadows I flourish, with wit that's a snare,
I'm the jester of roots, in this grand leafy lair!

Chants of the Early Blossom

Oh, the buds are all singing, what a hilarious show,
While I'm stuck down here, waiting for my glow.
They giggle and jingle, while I'm just a sprout,
Trying not to yell when the snails start to pout.

I wish I could giggle, so I practice each day,
But all that comes out is a leafish cliché.
They dance in the sunlight, while I watch from below,
Shouting, 'Hey blossoms, can I come to your show?'

The flowers just chuckle, 'You'll bloom in good time!'
As I plot my revenge, with a rhyme and a mime.
A little bit of patience, they say with a smirk,
While I search for a snail to turn grumpy to perk.

So I twiddle my leaves, practicing my jest,
To ensure when I bloom, I'll put them to the test.
With jokes in my petals, I'll be quite the delight,
And spring in my heart will make the frolics just right!

Dreams Woven in Green Threads

In the soil I wiggle, so snug and secure,
Where imaginations sprout, and daydreams endure.
I plan to be tall, to sway in the breeze,
But right now I'm just dodging insects with ease.

The sun makes a joke, I feel quite the fool,
With each little raindrop, I'm splashed like a pool.
My friends are the worms, they wiggle and squirm,
Sharing secrets of life, as we all take a turn.

I've envisioned a life in a forest of green,
With squirrels and birds, and a scene so serene.
Yet here in my patch, the cats think I'm prey,
I laugh, letting sunlight brighten my day.

But give me a chance, I'll stretch out my leaves,
With dreams that are grand, oh you best believe!
For now I'll just giggle, a sprout full of cheer,
One day, I'll be mighty, but right now I'm mere.

The Solitude of New Growth

Alone in the garden, the sun is my friend,
In shadows I giggle, on each twig I depend.
I ponder my future, the heights I might reach,
While chatting with ants, they're my favorite speech.

The breeze makes a joke, I sway with delight,
My limbs stretch out wide, oh, what a sight!
Yet every few hours, I'm in need of a drink,
I look to the sky, and of course, I just think.

"What if the rain comes, and I'm drenched like a sponge?

Will the weeds all complain? Shall we all live in grunge?"

I laugh at my worries, they're silly indeed,
Just a spindly green thing, with only one need.

To grow with a grin, with friends near and far,
Letting the sunlight guide me, that's how I spar.
In this soliloquy, so light and afloat,
I envision myself as a giant green goat!

The Awakening of Twigs

Awake little twigs, the morning is bright,
With dreams of the forest, oh what a sight!
I giggle and stretch, while shaking off dew,
If only the critters would share some tortilla stew.

Each chirp from the birds, a melody sweet,
In this funny old world, I'm the one with no feet.
Yet I see skyward, imagining flight,
Swinging with leaves, what a marvelous height!

So here I shall stand, with laughter and glee,
Through rain, wind, and sun, just a twinkling spree.
With my roots planted firmly, I shall rise and I'll sway,
I'll be the tall one who could've run away!

Sometimes I feel tiny, a mere little sprout,
Yet laughter's the key, without any doubt!
I'm more than just green; I'm a bright little star,
In the garden of life, I'm the best... by far!

Beauty in the Unseen Struggle

Beneath the surface, I dance with the weeds,
In silent debates, are they friends or just creeds?
I chuckle at molehills, they think they are grand,
While I'm here sprouting, oh isn't it planned?

My roots intertwine, like gossiping friends,
Together we chuckle, where the struggle transcends.
Each poke of my sprout, I learn how to thrive,
It's a comedy show, I'm just happy to jive.

With shadows of giants, I tiptoe with care,
Dancing on rays of light, as they flicker through air.
I might be small now, all twisted and curled,
But wait for the laughter to brighten this world!

So here's to the troubles that fuel my growth's rise,
I embrace all the pains—oh, they're such a surprise!
The beauty is subtle in this twisty game,
Each struggle I face whispers loud, "You are lame!"

Revelations of Resilient Growth

In the pot I sit so small,
Wishing I could have a ball.
Neighbors tease, they think I'm shy,
But my dreams stretch to the sky.

Roots dig deep, a twisty maze,
Entangled in this sunny phase.
Wiggling worms play peek-a-boo,
While I bloom, I'll start a zoo!

With sunlight's kiss, my leaves will dance,
And all the bugs will join in trance.
Giggling grasshoppers leap around,
In this leafy kingdom I have found.

Watch the clouds parade on high,
I'm just here with my leafy sigh.
Growing tall, I won't be beat,
I'll give those weeds a run, you bet!

The Life of a Leaf in Waiting

Hanging out on a branch so wide,
I daydream of the sunny tide.
Birds gossip of the great blue skies,
But here I am, it's no surprise.

With every breeze, I sway and tease,
A little twirl, I do with ease.
The squirrels snicker, but I must say,
I have my plans for a grand display!

Patience is key, or so they say,
While I wait to join the play.
When autumn calls, oh what a sight,
Red and gold, I'll take flight!

So for now, I shrug and grin,
Hurry up, let the fun begin!
Leaves may rustle, but I'll be bold,
A comedy in colors untold!

Ruminations in the Quiet Meadow

Among the blooms, I often muse,
Do daisies wear these fancy shoes?
Butterflies flutter by, oh so slick,
While I'm just waiting for my trick!

Tall thistles laugh with great delight,
They poke and prodded me all night.
But I dream up a clever scheme,
To outgrow them, oh, what a dream!

The ladybugs form a little crew,
Polishing shells, in their shades of hue.
I cheer them on, my leafy cheer,
Soon, it'll be my turn to premiere!

In this quiet meadow I'll take my stand,
Crack a joke, that's just my brand!
Growing greener, the joke's on them,
I'll burst forth—a leafy gem!

Tendrils of Tomorrow's Whisper

With tendrils curling, I begin to peek,
Eavesdropping on the flowers that speak.
Roots whisper secrets beneath the ground,
Oh, the tales of wonder that abound!

The wind rejoices, tickling my face,
I wiggle and giggle, just in case!
Rabbits hop by with stories galore,
Of digging tunnels and finding more.

Each inch I grow brings laughter bright,
A little green monster ready for flight!
My leaves will shimmer like a disco ball,
This garden party—oh, I'll enthrall!

So here's to tomorrow with a cheerful grin,
To all my friends, let the fun begin!
With each twist and turn, I'll find my way,
A vibrant life, come what may!

The Story of a Single Sprout

In a garden so small, I stand on my toes,
With dreams of a tree, as everyone knows.
I wiggle my leaves, I shout with delight,
'One day soon, I'll reach the sky so bright!'

The sun feels so warm, like a big friendly hug,
While raindrops are tickles, not a single bug.
I dance in the breeze with a leaf-shakin' cheer,
And wonder if squirrels will soon lend an ear!

Each day is a story, a little mix-up,
As I plan my big party for all the small buds.
"Bring snacks!" I proclaim, with a leaf-waving flair,
But they just respond with a quizzical stare.

So here I shall grow, with neighbors all round,
And laugh at the garden, a fun, leafy sound.
With life's little joys and its small little quirks,
I'll sprout in this patch, where all nature works.

A Luminary Among Shadows

In the garden of gloom, I stand out so bold,
With a tiny green body and dreams to behold.
My friends shout 'Sprout!' with a giggling tone,
But with all of this sunlight, I'm never alone!

Oh, the shadows of weeds, they tease me a lot,
They say, 'Look at you, just a twig on the spot!'
But wait till I flower, I'll show them my charm,
And maybe, just maybe, I'll elbow a warm!

I listen to whispers as sunbeams come in,
The voices of creatures darting around, quite a din.
"Let's throw a big bash!" I shout with a cheer,
But they roll on the ground, for they're full of good beer!

So here in this patch, I'll wriggle with glee,
Growing tall like a star, that's just right for me.
With laughter and light in the soil I now dwell,
I'll shine in the garden, and all will be swell!

Whispers of the Tender Shoot

Beneath moonlit skies, a tender shoot sighs,
'I'm ready to grow, but watch out for pies!'
The critters are sneaky, they nibble and munch,
With hopes of surviving this wild little brunch.

I witness the stars, they twinkle and chat,
'Look at our friend, what a curious brat!'
I giggle and wiggle my leaves in pure glee,
My dreams are much bigger than just being free.

Each day brings new tales from worms down below,
'Tell us your secrets,' they beg, 'come on, let us know!'
'Well, here's one secret,' I say with a grin,
'You're all in my salad—now that's a win!

So listen, dear friends, I'm growing so fast!
With each little leaf, I'm having a blast.
In the wild of the garden, I'm the star of the show,
With laughter surrounding, I'll keep stealing the glow!

Echoes in the Budding Grove

In the grove where I grow, I bounce like a ball,
With giggles of breezes that whisper and call.
While shadows pass by, I start to conspire,
To reach for the clouds, oh, that's my desire!

The wise old oak grumbles, 'You'll never make it!'
But he's just a bit grumpy, maybe needs a shake-it.
I'll be tall someday, stretching into the blue,
With roots like jazz hands, waving welcome to you!

As birds chirp their songs and the wind starts to dance,
I twirl and I giggle, it's my time to prance!
So gather 'round buddies, let's make some ruckus,
In a world full of greens, let's party and discuss!

So echo your laughter, let the good times roll,
In the budding grove, it's a bright, leafy stroll.
I'll rise with a spirit that's funny and free,
Just wait 'til you see the mighty tree I'll be!

The Heartbeat of a New Dawn

In the garden I bow low,
Trying to wiggle, not grow slow.
With each breeze, I sway and dance,
Yet tripping often, here's my chance.

The sun shouts, "Get up, little friend!"
While I giggle, my roots extend.
I chat with the bugs, they tell me tales,
Of brave little pebbles and funny snails.

My leaves wave like hands in the air,
Saying hi to the ants, without a care.
I ponder hopping, maybe I'll jump,
But a worm whispers, "You'll just thump!"

Oh, to be tall is quite the dream,
But for now, I'm just the punny green seam.
With laughter around, I grow and glow,
Sprouting jokes, as I steal the show!

Between Sky and Soil

Every raindrop whispers fun,
As I stretch toward the golden sun.
With my pals, the daisies, we play games,
Tagging shadows, we've got wild claims!

The clouds drift by in fluffy swirls,
Laughing at life, oh how it twirls.
I practice my flair, a leafy ballet,
And yelp at the bees that buzz my way!

"Hey, look at me, I'm reaching high!"
But I trip and tumble—oh my, oh my!
My roots hold steady, laughing a lot,
As I cartwheel through mud, from head to spot!

Life is rich, full of giggles and cheer,
Another sprout shouts, "Hey, let's persevere!"
With a wink to the moon, I will rise tall,
And turn every stumble into a ball!

Hope's Silent Blossom

Whispers of green tickle the air,
I dream of blooms, flashing flair.
"Watch me blossom!" I proudly declare,
But then the wind says, "Oh dear, beware!"

The squirrels gather, plotting their scheme,
To borrow my leaves for their wild dreams.
With my soft petals, I play my part,
Creating confetti straight from my heart!

The sun naps low, but I sing a tune,
Imagining daisies swirling with a moon.
"Just sprout your laughter, let it flow,"
Even the grumpy rocks start a show!

"Let's dance, oh roots! Keep this gig alive,"
Nature's party, we gleefully thrive.
And when I bloom, what a sight to see,
A comedy of colors, just wild and free!

A Young Sprout's Revelations

I wiggle my leaves, ready to share,
Confessions of growth, no time to spare.
The breeze tickles, I squeal with delight,
As earthworms grin, all set for a fight!

"Why grow straight?" I chime with a grin,
When squiggly lines can be where we begin.
The skies above giggle, the clouds puff out,
Laughing at sprout dreams that jump about!

"Who needs a ladder?" I quip to a bee,
When I can just stretch and reach for a tree!
With humor as fuel, I dream wide and grand,
No need to be serious; just grab the land!

So here I stand, with my roots in a twist,
Growing and giggling, I simply insist.
In this wild garden, humor reigns supreme,
Blossoming joy, fulfilling each dream!

www.ingramcontent.com/pod-product-compliance
Lightning Source LLC
Chambersburg PA
CBHW071814160426
43209CB00003B/90